Contents

Introduction

A confident communicator is someone who is natural and comfortable in various communication situations, including one-on-one, meetings, and presentations. Effective communication is crucial in business, we will help you boost your confidence. We will explore techniques to overcome public speaking fears, improve your vocal confidence, enhance body language, and manage speaking anxiety.

Enhance your listening skills, a crucial aspect of effective communication and leadership. This skill can benefit your career, help you make a positive impression on colleagues, and contribute to your success in various roles. Remember that listening is a learned behavior that can be improved with information, self-awareness, and practice. Embrace the opportunity to enhance your listening skills.

Every day presents conflicts due to competing interests, differing opinions, and challenging individuals. We will learn the process to navigate difficult situations, moving from conflict to cooperation. We will explore the name, blame, claim cycle and introduce the resolution roadmap—a versatile framework for conflict resolution. Practical examples will demonstrate skills like listening and asking diagnostic questions, empowering you to apply these abilities in your own conflict conversations. By promptly using these problem-solving skills, you can enhance your leadership potential significantly.

To elevate your career, embrace feedback as a crucial tool for development. Cultivate a feedback mindset involves effectively giving, receiving, and processing feedback, providing valuable insights for performance improvement and career advancement. We will explore how you handle feedback, examining internal narratives attached to it. Despite the potential emotional journey, your presence indicates readiness to uncover both strengths and areas for improvement. You will gain a deeper self-understanding and practical strategies for maintaining a feedback mindset.

How often have you experienced an immediate negative reaction to an email or text, possibly misinterpreting the message? In the modern workplace, expressing intentions and understanding others has become increasingly challenging. Despite the fact that 75% of face-to-face communication involves body language, a substantial 70% of team communication is now virtual. This shift has led to a significant empathy deficit, impacting innovative behaviors, trust, and overall satisfaction by up to 50%. To combat this loss of digital body language cues, it is crucial to adopt tools that enhance digital communication and foster healthier relationships with colleagues, bosses, clients, and even friends and family. Mastering these tools not only aids in completing tasks but also positions you as a proficient digital communicator.

Despite our well-meaning efforts, many attempts to influence others often fall short. Even with good intentions, supported by facts, deadlines, rewards, or penalties, success can be elusive. Drawing from extensive social science research worldwide, we will explore proven steps and methods to enhance your ability to influence others successfully, even in challenging situations.

Discovering instances of unintentional and intentional offensive remarks is not difficult. Well-intentioned individuals often make comments that lead to negative consequences, contributing to cultural conflicts worldwide. The challenge lies in addressing sensitive topics such as religion, social status, race, ethnicity, gender, politics, and ability without avoiding them altogether. We will guide you through these conversations, focusing on understanding and effective communication rather than promoting compliance or political correctness. We will explain why these topics can be challenging, share key principles, and provide strategies for engaging in constructive dialogues.

Mastering emotional intelligence can advance your career significantly. Emotionally intelligent communicators enhance organizational performance, cultivate strong relationships, and earn rewards. Learn key skills such as maintaining composure when upset, deciphering the unspoken dynamics of a room, responding adeptly to others' emotions, and expressing empathy. While intellect is valuable, your emotional quotient (EQ) can be even more beneficial for your career.

Learn to compose efficient emails. A study reveals employees invest over a quarter of their time in email-related activities. Optimize this investment by mastering the art of crafting purpose-specific and reader-friendly emails. Discover techniques for clear subject lines, effective wording, and proper formatting to enhance communication. Gain insights into using forwarding, copying, and blind copying strategically to foster relationships and maintain confidentiality. Upgrade your email skills for professional and impactful communication.

Chapter 1 Communicating with Confidence

What makes a good speaker?

A good communicator is not necessarily someone who speaks flawlessly without hesitation. Instead, it is about coming across as sincere and engaging. Charismatic and confident communicators draw people in and make them feel like they are having a one-on-one conversation, even in a large audience. Thoughtful language and genuine facial expressions and tone convey sincerity. Vulnerability, heartfelt stories, and meaningful experiences help establish a connection with the audience, making them listen and take action. A good speaker appears knowledgeable, engaging, and empathetic based on the context.

What holds people back?

Have you ever noticed how confident individuals can become nervous and disconnected when speaking in a group setting? What causes this shift from being an engaging conversationalist to a hesitant speaker in the spotlight? This anxiety often stems from primal instincts, where being the center of attention used to signal potential danger in our hunter-gatherer past. Public speaking can make us feel vulnerable, leading to concerns about making mistakes, boring the audience, or losing our place.

Various factors contribute to these speaking anxieties, such as setting high expectations for perfection, fearing challenges or disagreements from the audience, past negative experiences, and racing brain syndrome (RBS) where thoughts and speech are not in sync, causing nervousness.

Connecting with yourself

A common barrier to being a confident communicator is getting in our own way. Many people tend to communicate one-way, hurling words without connecting with the audience. This behavior creates an "endless loop trap," where ineffective communication patterns repeat. One-way communication disconnects us from others, making it all about ourselves.

To overcome this, we should slow down our thinking and focus on connecting with the audience. Begin each communication by considering how you want to be perceived. Instead of dwelling on anxiety, be mindful of words like confident, clear, engaging, or informative during the conversation. This approach helps you break free from self-doubt and anxiety, making the communication more effective.

Connecting with others

Connecting with others involves making the conversation about them, turning every significant interaction into a two-way exchange. This means delivering one thought at a time, whether it is a one-on-one discussion, a meeting, or a presentation. This approach slows down racing thoughts, keeps you focused on the moment, and allows you to gauge the audience's understanding. It also helps shift the focus away from yourself to the people you're speaking to.

For example, when making a request like doubling the marketing budget to the executive team, a one-way communicator might get caught in their head, worrying about various scenarios and reacting nervously to non-verbal cues. In contrast, a two-way communicator pays close attention to how the audience responds and can address concerns in real-time or later.

By delivering one thought at a time and being responsive to the audience, you create a meaningful connection and remain centered during the conversation.

Breathing properly

In stressful situations, especially when confidence is low, our breathing can become irregular. People often experience shallow or even held breath during nervous moments like meetings, presentations, or tough conversations. This shallow breathing deprives our bodies of oxygen, making it harder to think and concentrate, and leading to disorientation.

The reason for this is the release of stress-inducing hormones like cortisol and norepinephrine by the autonomic nervous system, which triggers the fight or flight response. When this happens, we need to stay calm and keep talking. Proper breathing can help soothe the nervous system.

One effective technique is Ujjayi breath, a form of diaphragmatic breathing. To stay calm and focused, exhale slowly through your nose while pulling in your belly, then inhale, allowing your belly to relax. Keep your chest still. Breathe in this way for three to five seconds per breath. This technique activates the vagus nerve, promoting relaxation and clear thinking. It may require practice to break old habits but can be beneficial for managing anxiety and improving your overall well-being.

Knowing what to say

Effective communication, especially in challenging or important situations, requires thorough preparation. Content quality is paramount because even the most confident communicator will be exposed without meaningful content. Every communicator needs clear, simple messages that are easy for everyone to understand, even non-native English speakers.

To create these messages, use simple words and short sentences. Avoid elongating sentences with conjunctions. Keep your points concise and separate them with periods. Structure your content thoughtfully to prevent a confusing jumble of ideas, which can make you appear unfocused and damage your credibility.

During preparation, identify your desired outcome and choose words that convey how you want to be perceived, whether as confident, inspiring, or another quality. Once you have determined these elements, you can organize your thoughts effectively.

Organizing your thoughts

For effective presentation preparation, use index cards to organize your thoughts. Start with a clear purpose: inform, persuade, or prompt action. Write your purpose on an index card labeled "purpose." Then, create three or four main ideas, each on separate index cards labeled "main idea." Add details to flesh out the main ideas, one per card. Your details should be concise and engaging.

Craft an engaging introduction that tells the audience why they should listen. Conclude with a memorable summary and a call to action. Arrange the index cards in this order: introduction, main ideas with their details, and conclusion. Speak naturally and confidently using the cards as a guide. For those who prefer using a text, the index card method provides a concise and coherent first draft of the presentation.

Making every word count

To effectively connect with others through words, choose your words thoughtfully and express them clearly. Words have a lasting impact, and we should make them count by using only important ones. Expressing words with meaning involves varying your tone, pace, volume, and inflection, just like when telling an engaging story. Even if you are not naturally connected to the content, emphasize at least one word in each sentence to sound engaged.

Enunciating every word can be challenging, especially for fast speakers. To improve clarity, do this exercise: place a pen or pencil gently between your teeth and read aloud, making sure to enunciate each word. After about a minute, remove the pen and continue reading. This exercise helps enhance your enunciation. Choosing words carefully, expressing them with meaning, and enunciating them clearly are the keys to making your words impactful.

Sounding confident

I want to address a common speech pattern called "uptalk," where sentences end with rising inflections, making statements sound like questions. Uptalk can diminish authority and confidence in speech, and it is more prevalent among young people. Linguist Robin Lakoff points out that women sometimes use "hedging" language and apologize excessively, which can undermine their speech. To improve your communication, vary your tone and inflection, avoid monotone speech, and consider standing while speaking for added energy. Experiment with different vocal tones and volumes in everyday conversations to engage your listeners more effectively.

Power of the pause

Many times, you might have experienced a fast-talking monotone speaker who does not hold your attention. Pauses can change the game, capturing the audience's attention and allowing for meaningful connections. For listeners, pausing is crucial because it gives them time to process what's said, particularly when something important is communicated. The length of a pause depends on the audience's engagement. From the speaker's perspective, pausing shows confidence and highlights the importance of what's being said. When delivering a message, it is beneficial to pause before and after most sentences, especially during significant points or when asking rhetorical questions. Using the word "pause" or "P" on index cards or notes serves as a reminder to slow down and add pauses while speaking.

Slowing down

If you tend to speak quickly, there are effective ways to slow down and communicate more deliberately. Instead of letting words blend together, elongate the vowel sounds in each word to help you connect with their meaning. Visualize your brain and tongue working together to maintain a focus on what you're saying as you say it, delivering one thought at a time. Avoid filling your speech with "uh" and "um," as these interruptions indicate a struggle for the right words and a lack of proper breathing. Instead, pause and take a breath when necessary to maintain articulateness. You can practice this with friends or colleagues by avoiding "uh" and "um," and this exercise can help you become a more deliberate and articulate speaker. Slowing down while speaking allows for better control, emphasizes important points, and builds anticipation in your audience, making your message more engaging.

Using your eyes

Observing a person's eye movements can reveal their emotions and thoughts. In public speaking, effective eye contact is vital for connecting with the audience and appearing confident. Rather than having restless eyes that make you appear nervous, focus on one person's face for each thought or idea, ensuring they've received the message before moving on. Extended eye contact during a powerful statement emphasizes your message. This approach helps you stay calm and conversational, even in large groups.

During a speech, aim to maintain eye contact at the beginning and end of each sentence, looking down at your notes as needed, but avoiding the appearance of reading. In everyday conversations, practicing meaningful eye contact can help build discipline and rapport. To improve eye contact skills, engage in a fun exercise called the "eye game." The objective is to deliver one thought to one face at a time, with participants lowering their hands when you establish direct eye contact and complete a thought. Use short sentences to enhance your eye contact and communication abilities.

Talking with your hands

Many people wonder whether they should use their hands when they speak, often resorting to letting them hang idly by their sides or in their pockets. However, talking with your hands can be quite beneficial. Gestures help you think and engage the audience. They make you more visually interesting, contributing to the 55% of communication conveyed through body language. Using your hands also adds inflection to your voice, making it more engaging and improving audibility, particularly for those with softer or monotonous speech. Effective hand gestures can project confidence and leadership. Clenching your fists is best avoided as it may convey nervousness or anger. Lastly, using purposeful hand movements can help dispel anxiety by making your speaking more dynamic and calming your nerves. Open fingers, slightly spread, with purposeful gestures can emphasize your points effectively.

Gesturing naturally

Using your hands when you speak might initially feel excessive, but it appears natural and exudes confidence to your audience. Avoid keeping your hands too close to your ribcage; maintain some distance. Occasionally, even when not speaking, having your hands in a forward position can display confidence. Adapt the motion of your hands to align with your message – employ a rolling gesture for progressions and side-to-side movements for comparisons. Crossed arms convey defensiveness. When aiming for a warmer tone or making a request, consider using an open-palms gesture, which is both reassuring and non-threatening. It is crucial not to overdo hand gestures. Unnecessary or repetitive motions, or gestures that do not align with your speech, can be distracting or even anxiety-inducing for your audience. While it is not necessary to have a gesture for every word, keeping your hands engaged contributes to your energy and effectiveness as a speaker. Practice using hand gestures from everyday interactions when addressing a group.

Managing facial expression

For your expressions to match your words and appear confident, use facial expressions effectively. Visualize the topic you are discussing to maintain a current focus and align your facial expressions with your message. Mismatched facial expressions can convey mixed messages. For example, saying "I'm very happy to be here" with an unsmiling face conveys inconsistency. Ensure your facial expressions reflect the mood, tone, and texture of your message, particularly through your eyes. Looking upward while speaking can make you seem uncertain. Conversely, looking down or to the side can give the impression of thoughtfulness. Genuinely smiling on cue can be challenging, but raising your eyebrows can help create a more natural smile. Recording yourself speaking can reveal areas for improvement in your facial expressions.

Handling nervousness

Effective management of body language is crucial to handling nervousness while speaking. Nervousness often manifests as body language leakage, including "tells" like speaking quickly, fidgeting, or using filler words. The "swallow" and "pursed lip" are common tells to watch for. Practicing a calm, grounded stance with shoulder-width feet can help alleviate nervous movement. Excessive blinking can make one appear anxious, so consciously controlling breathing can help. Shift the focus from being observed to observing your audience. Finally, when transitioning from a formal presentation to a Q&A, ask your own question to relax and speak more informally. Practice these strategies to manage your body language effectively.

Nervousness is common

It is natural to feel a little nervous when speaking in public. However, some people, including myself, experience more intense nervousness. To overcome my anxiety, I realized that I needed to take the pressure off myself. I stopped striving for perfection and embraced the idea that I, as the presenter, am not important. What I say and whether people understand it is what truly matters. I am merely the imperfect conduit for conveying information, and that perspective has freed me to focus on what is genuinely important.

Making fake confidence real

Have you ever heard the saying that sometimes the worst experience can turn out to be the best thing that ever happened to you? I found a way to transform fake confidence into real confidence within seconds by using bold hand and arm gestures during my speech. This approach allowed my brain to believe in my genuine confidence, and the result was one of the best presentations I ever delivered.

FAQs

I often receive questions about specific situations, such as, "What should I do if...?" Address some of these common inquiries and provide solutions.

1. What if I get flustered by a question?

   Use the "fluster strategy," which involves three steps:

   1. Breathe, as we often hold our breath when uncertain.

2. Say, "Excuse me" or "I beg your pardon" to request the question's repetition.

3. If still unsure, ask, "Please help me understand the context of the question" to gain more information for your response.

2. What if someone disagrees with me or doubts what I am saying?

Ask them questions to uncover the root of their concerns, showing openness to different opinions while building credibility for your argument.

3. What if my audience appears disinterested?

Pause for 3-5 seconds, breathe, and use silence as a powerful tool. Then, speak with more energy and animation, or consider allowing a short break.

4. What if someone is distracted by their phone during my talk?

Approach them and continue speaking nearby to regain their attention. Alternatively, consider that their distraction may not be related to your presentation.

5. What if I am interrupted while making a point?

Your response depends on the interrupter. If a colleague interrupts, politely ask for a few more seconds to finish your thought. Be open to interruptions that can enhance the conversation.

6. What if I am asked a question I cannot answer?

Express your commitment to accuracy and specificity, and inform them that you will provide the precise information later.

Wrap up

Every time you speak, use the communication techniques. Practice in various situations, like meetings or casual conversations. Start by focusing on one aspect at a time. Ensure you are breathing, emphasize words, maintain meaningful eye contact, embrace pausing, use hand gestures, and keep your sentences simple. Most importantly, speak and look like you mean it. You do not have to master everything at once. Gradually implement these techniques, such as improving eye contact one week, pausing the next, and so on. Practice confident communication in your everyday life.

Chapter 2 Effective Listening

Five skills for improved listening

Assess and enhance your listening skills by focusing on five key areas: recalling details, understanding the big picture, evaluating content, attending to subtle cues, and empathizing with the speaker. Rank these areas from your strongest to weakest, considering your ability to recall specific information, grasp overall meaning, judge content critically, interpret nonverbal cues, and empathize with emotional states.

Recall details

Recalling details involves retaining specific points made by a speaker, crucial for tasks like following complex instructions or acting on time-sensitive information. If improving this skill is a priority, follow the tips provided. Assess whether listening for details is appropriate by considering if you need to take immediate or future action based on the information. If not, focus on understanding the big picture or listening with empathy. To enhance detail recall, practice by listening to and remembering daily temperatures from a weather forecast without watching. Additionally, take notes during instructions for specific tasks, testing your recall by reviewing the notes or attempting the task. Improving this skill can save time, effort, and prevent potential oversights.

Understand the big picture

In some situations, getting caught up in details can be distracting, causing us to miss the broader scope or universal truth being communicated. For instance, in a meeting with a branding consultant, those focusing on the big picture asked strategic questions about implementation, research, and general direction, while others focused on specific details that were not yet relevant. Recognizing the appropriate time to focus on details is crucial. To improve your ability to understand the big picture, ask yourself how the information will impact the future and practice summarizing key ideas concisely. If you can distill complex ideas into a few sentences, you are mastering the skill of listening for the big picture.

Evaluate content

Daily, we often engage in evaluative listening, where we form opinions or make decisions based on gathered information. This type of critical listening is crucial in the workplace, ensuring the viability and future growth of organizations. Brenda and I experience it during student case competitions, where we assess the credibility, persuasiveness, and research quality of ideas. In the business world, critical listening is vital for making well-informed decisions. To excel at evaluative listening, focus on the content, assess the viability of arguments, and scrutinize the relevance and credibility of evidence presented. Avoid distractions and external factors. Practice by analyzing news or sports commentaries, comparing, contrasting, and deciding on the quality of presented information. Evaluative listening requires discipline and a concentration solely on content.

Attune to subtle cues

Attending to subtle cues involves reading nonverbal signals that convey additional meaning, especially in cultures where direct verbal communication is not the norm. It is crucial for effective listening, helping you adjust responses when verbal and nonverbal cues don't align. Subtle cues can be challenging to decipher, requiring observation and practice. Watching people converse in another language, analyzing television shows, or entering a meeting to discern hierarchies are practical exercises. If reading subtle cues is challenging, consider seeking a communication interpreter for context, culture, or people insights to enhance this essential listening skill.

Listen with empathy

Empathetic listening, while demanding time and energy, is invaluable for building relationships. It involves mirroring the speaker's emotions and body language, demonstrating a laser-focused attention that fosters trust and respect. In conflict situations or when dealing with colleagues, staff, or customers, empathetic listening is particularly important. Practice putting yourself in the speaker's shoes, immerse in the listening experience without judgment, and use acknowledging responses. Avoid discounting the speaker's feelings and refrain from phrases that minimize their emotions. Though emotionally draining, regular practice in less intense situations enhances empathetic listening skills, setting you apart as a communicator in both professional and personal contexts.

When and how to listen

Understanding the five types of listening and identifying your strengths and weaknesses is crucial. It is essential to choose the most appropriate listening type for different situations. In a workplace example, when addressing a conflict, empathetic listening is vital for building trust. Manager's lack of empathy leading to a heated exchange that could have been avoided with better listening. Another scenario involves a supervisor discussing a new project with an employee, emphasizing the importance of both recalling details and understanding the big picture. This underscores the significance of adapting your listening approach based on the context, even if you have a default listening style.

Getting distracted by internal noise

Listening attentively involves overcoming common challenges, including mental filters, multitasking, distraction by delivery, information overload, and inappropriate response. Mental filters, akin to filters in appliances, automatically process information but can lead to communication breakdowns if not clean. They develop from our experiences and beliefs, shaping how we perceive the world. For instance, doctors with different specialties had varied interpretations of a patient's foot pain until a nurse asked a simple question, revealing the true cause. Similarly, a visual example demonstrates how expectations influence perception. Emotional hot buttons and preconceived notions can cloud open listening, emphasizing the need to set aside assumptions for better understanding. Recognizing mental filters is crucial, especially if you catch yourself finishing sentences or preparing refutations mentally.

Multitasking

Multitasking, a significant obstacle to effective listening, is prevalent in today's connected world. Marshall Goldsmith emphasizes great listening as making the other person feel like the sole focus, a feat hindered by multitasking. Despite claims of efficient multitasking, research suggests it leads to errors and decreased productivity. Multitasking, while tempting, undermines the goal of being a good listener, necessitating intentional attention for effective communication.

Paying attention to delivery

Distractions related to a speaker's delivery can hinder effective listening. Whether it is counting filler words like "um" or addressing nonverbal distractions like spinach on teeth, it is crucial to refocus on the content. Rather than judging delivery, remind yourself that the goal is to learn from what is being said. For verbal distractions like soft-spoken individuals, mumbling, or accents, do not pretend to understand. Instead, ask for clarification or request the speaker to speak more clearly. Being a true listener involves focusing on understanding, not letting delivery obstacles impede the listening process.

Overwhelming yourself with information

Avoid the defeat of information overload with effective note-taking. While note-taking is beneficial, be selective to prevent falling behind. Depending on your purpose (learning or future action), focus on capturing the big picture or specific details. Handwritten notes are more effective than typing, according to a Princeton study. Choose a note-taking method that suits you and stick with it, choose brevity over lengthy sentences whenever possible.

Responding inappropriately

Avoid common response mistakes after listening. Steer clear of making it about yourself, criticizing, or providing unsolicited advice. Focus on the speaker's emotions, not just facts. Recognize and address your own listening challenges to enhance your overall listening skills.

Effective listening behaviors

After exploring common listening barriers, shift focus to positive responses that enhance listening skills. Effective responses include clarifying your role, using impactful nonverbals, respecting silence, paraphrasing for understanding, and mirroring the speaker's emotions. Evaluate and incorporate these behaviors into your action plan for improved listening.

Clarify your role

Your main role as a listener is to support the speaker according to their needs, whether it is providing advice, listening to them vent, or helping with analysis. If the speaker does not clarify their expectations, it is beneficial to clarify your role early in the conversation by asking questions like, "Do you want advice, or do you need me to just listen?" Understanding your information-processing preference, whether logic-focused or appreciation-focused, and communicating your role accordingly enhances effective listening.

Use nonverbal cues

The widely cited statistic by UCLA psychologist Albert Mehrabian states that 93% of communication is emotional, conveyed through nonverbals like tone and body language. As an active listener, short affirmations like "Mm-hmm" suffice to express attentiveness, especially during phone conversations. In addition to tone and brief words, nonverbal responses like facial expressions, eye contact, and personal space contribute significantly to effective listening. These cues, such as smiling, maintaining eye contact, and adjusting personal space, play a vital role in conveying engagement and openness. Recording and reviewing your nonverbal behaviors can provide valuable feedback for improvement. Given that the majority of communication is nonverbal, paying attention to these aspects enhances your effectiveness as a listener.

Allow silence

Silence plays a crucial role in effective listening, as noted in the quote, "The quieter you become, the more you can hear" by Ram Dass. Physical silence involves refraining from fidgeting or shifting positions, indicating focused attention on the speaker. For kinesthetic processors who naturally move while processing information, sitting still enhances the perception of attentive listening, especially in face-to-face interactions. Taking notes can also aid concentration, but it is essential to seek permission, considering the context. Vocalics, such as strategic pauses, affirming nods, and maintaining eye contact, contribute to effective listening. In certain cultures, like Korean, Chinese, and Japanese, silence is valued as a sign of respect, showcasing the cross-cultural significance of incorporating silence into listening practices.

Paraphrase what was said

Paraphrasing involves summarizing a message with fewer words, signaling attentive listening and ensuring accurate understanding. This active listening technique is valuable in conflict resolution or any situation where clarification is needed. Phrases like "So you're saying that..." or "Can I take a minute and tell you what I've heard so far?" help to refocus the conversation and prioritize key points. Practicing paraphrasing and clarification lines enhances active listening and adds value to conversations.

Match emotions

Active listening involves not only matching but also mirroring the speaker's enthusiasm, concern, or seriousness through physical reactions. This includes aligning posture, gestures, speech pacing, vocabulary choices, volume, tone, and speech patterns. Mirroring builds rapport and cohesion, contributing to effective communication. However, in challenging situations, like dealing with a difficult customer, mirroring the speaker's emotion may not be advisable; instead, using congenial body language and open posture can help defuse tension.

Effective listening in action

Evaluate yourself and your peers. How often do you encounter appropriate paraphrasing or effective emotion matching? Identifying these behaviors is the initial step toward becoming an exceptional listener. The next challenge is to practice these skills in diverse settings, such as weddings, family gatherings, or staff meetings, demonstrating your commitment to attentive listening through both words and actions.

Chapter 3 Conflict Resolution Foundations

Play the name, blame, and claim game

Conflict is a constant in human relationships due to conflicting wants, needs, goals, and values. This arises from imbalances in resource access and differing opinions on societal rules. The name, blame, claim cycle occurs when one believes they are deprived of something, attributes it to someone else, and sees it as a violation of a value or rule. For instance, if Mike excludes his manager Linda from an email, conflict arises as Linda feels deprived, blames Mike, and claims a violation of workplace norms. Reflect on your own conflicts by identifying what you feel deprived of (name), who you blame (blame), and the violated value or rule (claim).

Understanding conflict styles

Our response to conflict is shaped by our upbringing and culture. To enhance conflict resolution skills, understanding our default conflict response style is crucial. The Thomas-Kilmann Conflict Model outlines different styles, such as Avoid, Accommodate, Compete, Collaborate, and Compromise. Identifying your default style is key. For example, in the Avoid quadrant, fear of rejection prevents you from asking for a promotion, resulting in a loss for both you and your team. Collaborate, positioned at the center of the model, is suggested as an effective approach for finding win-win solutions. By entering conversations with the goal of mutual understanding and exploring options, you can preserve and deepen relationships. Recognizing your default style allows you to choose collaboration as a more effective problem-solving method.

Recognizing contentious tactics

When we perceive unfair treatment or neglect of our needs, we often react with contentious tactics to resolve conflict, such as ingratiation, promises, persuasive argumentation, shaming, threats, and physical force. While these tactics may offer short-term gains, overuse can erode relationships and lead to future conflicts. Recognizing these tactics as signals of underlying issues allows for a pause and an opportunity to identify unmet needs or concerns. By asking questions and digging deeper, one can shift from blame to cooperation, potentially avoiding full-blown conflicts.

Unwinding cognitive bias

Examine cognitive biases, universal thoughts that influence our judgment during disagreements. In conflict, these biases operate beneath our awareness, causing us to cling stubbornly to our positions. Hindsight bias leads us to see past events as predictable, hindering problem-solving. Fundamental attribution error makes us attribute others' behavior to personality defects, overlooking situational influences. Confirmation bias leads us to interpret information in a way that confirms our preconceptions, limiting a holistic view. Belief bias involves forming opinions based on the belief in the truth or falsity of a conclusion rather than its merits. While biases are inherent, recognizing them allows for a step back, fostering awareness and opening room for different perspectives, ultimately diffusing or avoiding conflicts.

Identifying issues and needs

The resolution roadmap, a five-step framework for conflict resolution, starts with identifying issues and needs. In a blaming mindset, acknowledging and discussing the conflict can be challenging but is crucial for progress. To move beyond blame, self-reflection is necessary. Consider the nature of the disagreement: relational, substantive, or perceptual. For instance, in a work scenario like Mike and Linda's, Mike recognizes a process disagreement and a relational issue with Linda. Investigating personal needs and behaviors is the next layer. Mike reflects on his actions, realizing he is not committed to the project but desires to share ideas for the best outcome. Exploring deeper, he also seeks autonomy and recognition. Understanding motives allows for positive actions to address the conflict, turning away from blame and towards resolution. The first resolution roadmap step focuses on recognizing and understanding personal motives without assigning blame.

Distinguishing fact from fiction

In conflicts, there is a distinction between facts and interpretations, known as the second step in the resolution roadmap. Consider a scenario with Mike and Linda: the fact is Mike submits a proposal to Linda, and she provides edits. The fiction arises when Mike interprets this as lack of appreciation, leading to the name, blame, claim cycle. Trouble arises not from facts but from the stories we tell ourselves about them. The fact from fiction exercise involves five questions to examine and clarify these stories and feelings. Question one assesses your behavior on the issue. Question two explores the stories justifying your behavior. Question three identifies the feelings generated by these stories. Question four encourages finding alternative perspectives. Question five emphasizes taking responsibility, not blame, for your part in the conflict. While challenging, this practice provides clarity for returning to cooperation and workability.

Opening the conflict conversation

Opening a conflict resolution conversation, the third step in the resolution roadmap, can be challenging. However, the clarity gained from self-investigation allows you to move from avoidance to conversation. To open successfully, state the facts, present your story as your perspective, and ask for your partner's viewpoint. In an example between Wilson and Gloria, Gloria addresses issues with Wilson's leadership style. Despite resistance, Gloria persists in stating facts, telling her story, and asking questions. Not everyone may possess the same conflict resolution skills, but persistence and calm communication can create a safe space for both perspectives to emerge.

Gaining alignment and brainstorming

Step four in the resolution roadmap involves gaining alignment and brainstorming, a critical stage in the framework for solving everyday problems. Rather than rushing into solutions, which may lead to false consensus, it's essential to navigate the messy part of hearing the other person's perspective and ideas. The "big deal question" helps in this process—asking what everyone is committed to or the shared goal. In an example between Gloria and Wilson, staying focused on exceeding targets and protecting the team helps find solutions during the messy part of the conversation. By answering the big deal question, you can bring shape and focus to brainstorming, shifting from self-centered outcomes to shared purpose in conflict resolution.

Getting to agreement

The fifth step in the resolution roadmap, a framework for solving everyday problems, is reaching agreement. Contrary to the belief that it is an easy step, it is crucial to avoid skipping over what both parties are actually agreeing to. This is illustrated in an example between Gloria and Wilson. After discussing key points, they define and commit to specific accountabilities and next steps. By being diligent about identifying next steps and specifying the details (what, who, and by when), conflicts can be prevented from recurring.

Increasing your conflict capacity

Listing five behaviors you would like to change in yourself, especially when observed in others. Then, consider a recent argument and identify the trigger. Rate the intensity on a scale of one to ten and assess your capacity to deal with those feelings. For instance, if your boss takes credit for your work (trigger), and you rate a nine in intensity but a three in capacity, it indicates a significant gap. To bridge this gap, focus on the first two steps of the resolution roadmap—identifying issues and distinguishing fact from fiction. Afterward, let some time pass to cool off before approaching the conversation. If uncertain, practice with a friend through role-playing to build confidence in addressing conflicts. Remember, conflict resolution is about personal discipline and practices for self-transformation, emphasizing that change starts with ourselves, not others.

Asking diagnostic questions

The crucial practice in conflict resolution is asking open-ended or diagnostic questions, starting with who, what, when, where, how, and why. Research by social psychologist Adam Galinsky reveals that 93% of people overlook the power of diagnostic questions, which can significantly impact outcomes. Closed-ended questions often yield yes or no answers, hindering dialogue. In contrast, diagnostic questions, like those used by Gloria, a senior director of engineering, open doors for exploration and uncovering real issues. When facing resistance, persist, slow down, and ask more diagnostic questions, as "no" is part of the journey to "yes." A powerful tip is to pause and rephrase close-ended questions into open-ended ones using "what" or "how" to enhance communication.

Listening

In conflict resolution, after initiating the conversation and asking diagnostic questions, the next crucial step is to cultivate curiosity and practice effective listening. There are three levels of listening. Level one is self-oriented, level two involves focused attention on the conflict partner, and level three, global listening, taps into intuition to grasp unspoken issues related to the shared purpose. In an example with Gloria, a senior engineering director, she demonstrates calm and measured listening skills, even in the face of arrogance from Wilson. To enhance your listening ability, eliminate distractions, be present, make eye contact, and provide verbal and non-verbal cues. Reflect what you hear to clarify and understand your conflict partner's perspective. Effective listening is essential for successful conflict resolution and minimizes the likelihood of revisiting conflicts in the future.

Labeling, mirroring, and silence

In conflict resolution, three tactical listening skills—labeling, mirroring, and silence—contribute to building tactical empathy, a concept coined by Chris Voss. Labeling involves reframing your conversation partner's perspective by starting with phrases like "it sounds like" or "it seems like" and naming their dominant feelings, interests, or perspective. In an example with Gloria, a senior engineering director, labeling helps uncover and name her boss Wilson's perspective, facilitating a more productive conversation.

The second skill, mirroring, entails repeating the last few or critical words of your partner's language, especially useful when confused or triggered. In the interaction between Gloria and Wilson, mirroring assists in defusing conflict and maintaining a constructive dialogue.

The third skill is silence, which proves beneficial when unsure how to respond or when a partner's statement requires a cooling-off period. Gloria strategically uses silence to address Wilson's statement, "Look, I'm irritable and in a hurry," allowing for a more engaged conversation.

Incorporating these tactical listening skills into everyday conversations—listening, labeling, mirroring, and using silence—can help guide conflicts toward resolution.

Reframing

Framing, or how we describe a problem, plays a crucial role in conflict resolution. Just like changing the frame on a picture alters our perception, reframing conflict can bring parties together. Cognitive biases and stories often blind us during conflict, making reframing challenging. We focused on communication skills like asking diagnostic questions, paraphrasing, labeling, and mirroring. These skills benefit conflict resolution by understanding partners' interests, checking understanding, signaling disruptive statements, and building empathy. Labeling and mirroring are tactical empathy skills that act as reframing tools. To deepen understanding, diffuse negative statements to find workability. Wayne Dyer's insight holds: "If you change the way you look at things, the things you look at change." Practice reframing by identifying and transforming negative statements into a more positive light.

Next steps and resources

Having a past means we are susceptible to triggers and conflicts, often labeling others as difficult or manipulative. Despite their actions, the mantra remains: it is never solely about the other person. When conversations take a negative turn, pause and help identify real issues and needs. Embrace failure as a chance to learn and improve. Recommended books for further insight: "Why Won't You Apologize" by Harriet Lerner, "Never Split the Difference" by Chris Voss, and "Crucial Conversations" by Kerry Patterson and Joseph Grenny. Possessing the tools is not enough; mastery comes through choosing and practicing them in everyday conflict resolution.

Chapter 4 Developing a Feedback Mindset to Accelerate Your Career

What's your feedback relationship status?

Similar to romantic relationships, you have a unique connection with feedback that influences your behavior. Explore the four feedback relationship statuses:

1. It's Complicated: A love-hate relationship; value feedback but struggle to let go of mistakes.

2. It's Just the Way I Am: Minimal engagement with feedback, embracing a fixed mindset; avoids growth work.

3. It's Not You, It's Me: Toxic relationship; self-critical, doubts abilities, struggles with self-esteem.

4. It's Official: Healthy relationship; embraces a growth mindset, learns from feedback, focuses on self-improvement.

Reflect on your typical response to constructive feedback to gain insight into your feedback relationship status, recognizing that it can evolve over time.

Examine your emotional response to feedback

Feedback, much like a roller coaster, can evoke various emotions. It is crucial to develop emotional literacy to navigate this roller coaster effectively. The first step is identifying the emotional response, naming the feelings during or after feedback. Understanding what these emotions convey is essential; they offer valuable information about oneself. In a feedback conversation, if feeling nervous or defensive, ask why and explore the source of these emotions for self-discovery. The next step is to respond intentionally, recognizing that negative feelings are messengers, not inherently bad. Taking control of emotional responses empowers a positive experience on the feedback roller coaster and ensures a picture at the end that one can be proud of.

Unpack your feedback baggage

If you often feel tense or hold your breath during feedback conversations due to negative past experiences, you might be carrying "feedback baggage." This baggage, linked to poorly delivered feedback, can impede personal and professional growth. To unload this baggage, start by identifying the most painful feedback, examining its impact on your journey, and then consciously letting it go. Write down three reasons why the feedback was wrong or symbolically discard it. Repack what is necessary by replacing negative thoughts with positive ones through visualization, empowering yourself for growth. Embrace vulnerability, introspection, honesty, and commitment to reclaim control over your development. Unpack that baggage and move forward.

The importance of processing feedback

Effectively processing feedback is crucial for personal growth and reaching your potential. It involves analyzing the internal narrative tied to the feedback you receive, as our self-talk is powerful. Reflect on your thoughts and feelings to gauge whether you are processing feedback positively. Override negative thoughts with more productive ones, focusing on improvement rather than self-criticism. Emphasize learning from the feedback, recognizing its value and potential for growth. Visualize success to create a positive image of your capabilities. Use these strategies to enhance your ability to process feedback and leverage it for future success.

Control the feedback narrative

It is crucial to manage the narratives we attach to feedback. The first step is identifying the facts—truths about the events, not our interpretations. In my case, being a first-generation college student receiving extensive feedback was a fact. Next, recognize the narrative you have developed, distinguishing it from facts. Finally, rewrite the narrative by replacing negative interpretations with positive, fact-based affirmations. Remember, there is no perfect way to do this—focus on grounding narratives in facts and creating positive stories.

Use the SIFT model

The SIFT model is a prioritization tool for managing feedback overload. SIFT stands for source, impact, frequency, and trends.

1. Source: Consider the person providing feedback. Trusted contacts, acquaintances, and strangers have different weights in prioritizing feedback.

2. Impact: Evaluate the impact of feedback on yourself, others, or projects. Categorize it as large, medium, or small based on the severity of impact.

3. Frequency: Examine how often you have received the feedback. Differentiate between frequent, occasional, or first-time feedback to gauge the prevalence of the behavior.

4. Trends: Identify patterns in feedback across various aspects of your life, such as work, home, or school. Determine if the feedback has a widespread or isolated presence.

Using the SIFT model helps individuals gain clarity on prioritizing feedback by breaking it down into manageable components. Applying this model allows for a more structured approach to address feedback and make meaningful improvements.

Naming the feedback

Feedback is not uniform; it falls into three categories: constructive, destructive, and reinforcing. Constructive feedback centers on actions, guiding you toward future possibilities. It feels supportive and propels you towards growth. Destructive feedback, on the other hand, focuses on the person, dwelling on past actions and limitations, often feeling judgmental. This feedback can be discouraging and impact performance, self-esteem, and belonging. Reinforcing feedback emphasizes your present strengths, acting as cornerstones anchoring you in your gifts. It encourages appreciation for what you excel at and provides balance alongside constructive feedback. Evaluate feedback by considering whether it addresses actions, the person, or strengths, determining if it is a stepping stone, throwing stones, or a cornerstone. This approach helps respond to feedback in a way that enhances career success.

Solicit feedback

Feedback is not uniform; it falls into three categories: constructive, destructive, and reinforcing. Constructive feedback centers on actions, guiding you toward future possibilities. It feels supportive and propels you towards growth. Destructive feedback, on the other hand, focuses on the person, dwelling on past actions and limitations, often feeling judgmental. This feedback can be discouraging and impact performance, self-esteem, and belonging. Reinforcing feedback emphasizes your present strengths, acting as cornerstones anchoring you in your gifts. It encourages appreciation for what you excel at and provides balance alongside constructive feedback. Evaluate feedback by considering whether it addresses actions, the person, or strengths, determining if it is a stepping stone, throwing stones, or a cornerstone. This approach helps respond to feedback in a way that enhances career success.

Solicit feedback from your manager

Feedback is a crucial aspect of your career development, shedding light on strengths and potential obstacles. Regularly seeking input from your manager allows you to enhance or maintain performance before formal reviews. Studies reveal that those who seek feedback tend to receive higher performance ratings. When approaching your manager for feedback, choose a dedicated time and place for a focused discussion. Clearly define the areas you seek feedback on, whether specific projects, skill progress, goal status, or career advancement. Send your manager a heads-up beforehand to set the tone and facilitate thoughtful responses. During the meeting, seek a balance of constructive and positive feedback by asking what to start, stop, or continue. This ensures a well-rounded approach to growth. Ask follow-up questions, take notes, and express gratitude afterward. Sending a summary of takeaways or action steps reinforces your commitment to feedback and growth. This intentional approach ensures that each feedback conversation fuels optimism and energy in your career journey.

Source feedback from team meetings

Teamwork is crucial for success, and the same applies to personal growth. Adopting a team approach to feedback enhances collective wisdom. Seeking feedback from your team is vital for professional development, fostering real-time learning and relationship-building skills. Here are key questions to ask during team meetings for meaningful feedback:

1. "What are your thoughts?" - Encourages intellectual inclusion and diverse contributions. Note similarities and differences for valuable insights.

2. "What have we not considered?" - Prompts deep thinking to uncover potentially missed aspects, minimizing risks and preventing roadblocks.

3. "What is our next step?" - Assesses team readiness to progress, revealing areas that need further attention or adjustment for improved future meetings.

Inform your team in advance about these questions to facilitate readiness and contribution, creating a sense of belonging, psychological safety, and unlocking collective wisdom.

Gather feedback at project completion

In project teams, diverse experiences contribute to success. Utilizing feedback from your team enhances future projects. Consider adopting after-action reviews, a framework originating from the U.S. Army and widely used for reflection and learning. Here are key steps:

1. Introduce the Idea Early: Socialize after-action reviews at the project's start to prepare the team and encourage active observation of strengths and areas for improvement.

2. Schedule the Review: Ensure the after-action review is on the calendar to prioritize its importance amid project tasks.

3. Ask Four Key Questions:

   a. What were our expectations?

   b. What actually occurred?

   c. What went well and why?

   d. What can we improve and how?

4. Follow Up and Follow Through: Summarize feedback, allow additions, and implement improvements in subsequent projects. Share insights with other leaders for collective learning and continued success.

Give the GIFT of feedback

To deliver effective feedback, use the GIFT framework:

1. G: Give the Feedback

   - Commit to sharing feedback for growth.

   - Ask if the feedback can help improve, avoid negative impact, and influence the future.

   - Consider if you'd want the feedback in their position.

2. I: Intention Check

   - Assess your intentions, affecting tone, body language, and overall impact.

   - Check your feelings, perspective, and speech to align intention with impact.

3. F: Focus the Feedback

   - Concentrate on one to two specific behaviors for clarity and effectiveness.

   - Ensure the feedback is behavior-focused, allowing for meaningful improvement.

4. T: Time

   - Deliver feedback promptly for maximum impact.

   - Even if delayed, providing feedback is better than withholding it indefinitely.

By following this framework, you can offer a valuable gift of feedback that positively influences someone's career trajectory.

Develop feedback channels

To address this feedback gap, it is crucial to diversify feedback channels. Here are four channels to tap into:

1. Customer Feedback:

  - Use customer satisfaction surveys or testimonials.

  - Directly access feedback on the impact of your product or service.

2. Cocreator Feedback:

  - Engage in one-on-one check-ins or group debriefs.

  - Gain insight into technical and interpersonal skills from those you collaborated closely with.

3. Champion Feedback:

  - Provide project status updates to champions.

  - Discuss with individuals who understand and have a vested interest in your work.

4. Challenger Feedback:

  - Seek opinions that challenge your thinking, even unpopular ones.

  - Find individuals who can play devil's advocate and offer diverse perspectives.

While manager feedback is crucial, expanding your feedback sources to customers, cocreators, champions, and challengers enhances your growth opportunities and ensures a more comprehensive evaluation of your performance.

Give yourself feedback

To enhance personal growth and development, schedule reflection time on your calendar, choosing a frequency that aligns with your needs. Writing down reflections is crucial; draw a line down the center of a paper to list gifts on the left and gaps on the right. Acknowledge and celebrate your wins, noting what you did well. Reflect on challenges faced, focusing on growth areas without self-criticism. Close the reflection by considering what you learned, how to leverage strengths, address gaps, and use the insights moving forward. Mastering self-feedback empowers you to navigate external feedback more effectively, fostering a journey of self-discovery and development.

Chapter 5 Digital Body Language

New signals and devices

Understanding the significance of nonverbal communication, including body language, is crucial for interpreting meaning. While in-person interactions are not always feasible, it's essential to grasp the new signals of digital body language to connect effectively with colleagues. These digital body language signals encompass word choice, response time, email signatures, recipients, communication mediums, punctuation, and more. To use these signals effectively, ask yourself three key questions: Did I provide enough context in my message? Am I conveying the right emotional tone? Is there a clear call to action or next step? These questions will enhance your understanding and utilization of digital body language signals.

Brevity creates confusion

Office workers receive an average of 120 emails daily, responding to around 60 of them. In the rush to communicate quickly, messages often lack context, leading to confusion or strained relationships. A story from Adrian, an advertising agency team leader, illustrates the impact of unclear communication. Sending a brief meeting invitation, Adrian unintentionally caused anxiety for Bob, who thought he was about to be fired. It is crucial to differentiate between a brief and a clear message in digital body language. Bosses and managers can foster clarity by asking three questions: Am I clear about my needs? Did I include the right people? Am I intentional about response expectations? Using clear acronyms, like NNTR (no need to respond), helps prevent brevity-induced confusion and anxiety, ensuring effective communication.

Assume best intent when communicating

In daily communications, deciphering messages can be challenging. Misinterpretations are common, leading to frustration. Practicing digital grace involves prioritizing empathy and assuming positive intentions. For instance, a client's delayed responses were initially perceived as laziness, but later, it was revealed that her boss did not respond to emails promptly. The lesson is to assume positive intentions first, confirm interpretations, and give people the benefit of the doubt. Shifting conversations to a different medium and having open-ended discussions with a curious tone can foster understanding and clarity in challenging situations.

Respond carefully to digital messages

In our fast-paced communication era, errors and typos can abound, leading to wasted time and energy in corrections. To enhance understanding and trust-building, it is crucial to practice patience and respond carefully. Reading and rereading responses, considering potential misinterpretations, and scheduling communication for optimal engagement times are key strategies. Taking a moment before sending important messages allows for clarity, power, and perspective, fostering trust and connection with colleagues, regardless of distance.

All channels are not created equal

Utilizing multiple communication channels can enhance efficiency, but misusing them may impact trust and branding. Establishing norms for when and why to use different mediums is crucial. Consider four key factors: length, complexity, familiarity, and discipline. Tailor your choice of channel based on the message's length, complexity, your relationship with the recipient, and the message's confidentiality. Exercise discipline to avoid redundancy and prioritize empathy, respecting others' time and privacy. Establishing clear channel etiquette in your team fosters effective communication and removes barriers to productivity.

Communicate your feelings

Expressing authentic feelings in digital communication can be challenging, but four effective digital body language signals can help: exclamation marks, periods, question marks, and emojis. Exclamation points convey urgency, excitement, or enthusiasm, with varying intensity based on the number used. Periods can signal anger or convey a less sincere tone, especially in multiple periods. Question marks, depending on quantity, indicate genuine interest, confusion, frustration, or anger. Emojis, with their varied expressions, are powerful cues for conveying tone. Being conscious of emotional tone enhances communication and collaboration in digital interactions.

Negotiating power dynamics

In digital communication, masking anger in passive-aggressive messages is common. Deciphering the true meaning behind phrases like "per my last email" or "gentle reminder" can be challenging. Power dynamics, including bullying and micromanagement, are prevalent, leading to questions about power distribution and trust levels in relationships. The Power and Trust Matrix, assessing power (up or down) and trust (close or far), guides the use of digital body language signals. For instance, brevity may be suitable for messages to junior reports (up/close), while longer explanations and thoughtfulness may be prioritized for situations with lower trust levels (down/far). Understanding the matrix helps improve communication by aligning digital body language signals with the dynamics of power and trust.

Take charge of your communication

Here is a guide to becoming a master digital communicator:

1. Understand power dynamics and trust levels in your situation.

2. Consider the positive intent behind messages before reacting negatively.

3. Seek clarity when messages are brief or confusing.

4. Use the right communication channel, considering implications and priorities.

5. Learn from your responses over time, adopting perspectives of others.

6. Establish digital body language norms in your team to enhance clarity and reduce confusion.

By following these steps, you can become a digital body language guru and master collaboration.

Chapter 6 Influencing Others

Find inspiration

Think of someone in your life who profoundly influenced you positively, such as a parent, coach, teacher, or friend. Choose one and answer four questions: 1) Who is this person, and why do you consider them a significant positive influencer? 2) What specific actions or words were particularly meaningful? 3) How did their influence impact you and your life? 4) Moving forward, what can you do for yourself and others to honor this person's contribution? This reflective activity, based on research, reveals a powerful positive influence tool. Interviews with influential individuals highlight the impact of inspirational figures from their past. By keeping these role models in mind, effective influencers draw motivation and inspiration, seeing influence as a way of being, not just a means to an end. This approach, rooted in honoring legacies, turns inspiration-based influence into a lifelong gift.

Build rapport

To enhance your influence, focus on building rapport and trust. When dealing with people, especially those you have a connection with, willingly contribute extra effort. Actively listen, show understanding, and ask individuals about their desired outcomes in conversations or projects. Proactively build rapport by learning about others, as demonstrated in a study where pairs with personal information reached impasses only 6% of the time compared to 29% without rapport. Prioritize positive intent by stating your purpose upfront and connecting it to shared values. Acknowledge others' positive intent explicitly, especially in challenging conversations, to avoid misunderstandings. Protect trust by confirming positive intent before addressing concerns, fostering a collaborative atmosphere rather than hitting unnecessary impasses. Building relationships and trust with influencers is key to achieving persuasive goals.

Be likable

To maximize influence, consider both your message and your likability as the messenger. Authenticity is key—do not fake it, find your genuine likable qualities. Adopt a positive mindset, emphasizing your happiness to be present. Identify similarities, especially rare ones, and use inclusive language like "we" to strengthen connections. Highlight positive qualities sincerely, framing compliments as questions for authenticity. Credit individuals with qualities relevant to your priorities to influence their mindset positively. Aim to be in the group that causes happiness, appreciating and showcasing likable qualities in others to enhance your influence.

Be influenceable

Tony Hsieh, the founder and CEO of Zappos.com, emphasizes the importance of being influenceable. He defines humility as thinking of oneself less, not thinking less of oneself. Being influenceable means being open-minded and open-hearted without compromising principles. Instead of winning arguments, focus on winning hearts and minds, avoiding the trap of making it about winning or losing. Acknowledge others' contributions positively and confidently express how their input affects you. Share a quality you're working to improve, demonstrating authenticity and inviting collaboration. Influence is not just about getting your way; it is about earning your way into people's hearts and minds to create positive change.

Turn objections into actions

Effective influencers do not take objections personally; they see them as motivation. Recognizing that different perspectives exist, they embrace objections as clues, not obstacles. Instead of avoiding objections, they actively explore them to understand better. The goal is to turn objections into actions. Rather than resisting objections, treat them as invitations to learn and transform them into opportunities for positive actions. Embrace objections and turn challenges into opportunities for influence and success.

Think long term

In influence attempts, there is more at stake than immediate results; the impact on relationships and reputation matters. The best influencers prioritize both short-term results and long-term implications. They aim for results while also nurturing relationships and preserving their reputation. The daily relationships and reputation test—focusing on building relationships and positive reputation—helps guide interactions for better immediate results and lasting positive influences.

Simple, specific, and surprising

To enhance the persuasiveness of your ideas, ensure they are simple, specific, and surprising. Simplify your core message, as demonstrated by a successful technical presentation turning water flow theory into the ability to wash clothes and shower simultaneously. Make your message surprising by presenting insights in an attention-getting or unexpected manner. For example, a session on organizational values became memorable when a young refugee shared the story behind her grandmother's necklace. Incorporate these three elements—

simplicity, specificity, and surprise—to amplify the impact of your persuasive message.

Credible sources

Enhance your persuasive power by citing credible sources, such as reputable institutions like top research centers, prestigious universities, or foundations. You can also quote individuals with strong credentials or high standing in your organization. The credibility of the institution or person you cite strengthens your persuasive impact. For instance, referencing experts like Robert Cialdini in the field of influence adds significant weight to your approach. To effectively employ this strategy, identify leading experts and institutions on your topic, summarize their insights, and choose the most persuasive ones for your situation. Citing credible sources is a win-win, giving credit to others while bolstering your persuasive message.

Urgency and scarcity

Create urgency or scarcity to boost motivation, as opportunities with clear near-term limits are more compelling. For instance, Colleen Zodd, a successful infomercial writer, increased urgency by altering the tagline from "Operators are waiting; please call now" to "If operators are busy, please call again." This implied high demand, resulting in a significant increase in calls and sales. To implement this strategy: First, emphasize the need to act immediately, explaining the consequences of waiting. Second, highlight limitations on resources, information, or supplies. Third, leverage the power of loss by clarifying what will be missed if action is not taken. Utilize urgency to prompt action before it is too late.

Pain and gain framing

Illustrate pain and gain in your communication. People are highly motivated by penalties, rewards, losses, and profits—both negative and positive implications. Emphasize the avoidance of losses, as individuals are generally two to three times more motivated to prevent a loss than to seek a gain. For example, additional fees in transactions exploit this tendency, as people are reluctant to abandon the time and effort invested. To effectively utilize this strategy: First, identify the concerns, risks, headaches, or problems your recommendation alleviates. Second, emphasize the specific pains and gains most relevant to your audience. Use this approach to minimize pain and maximize gain in your communication.

Compare and contrast

Enhance your persuasive impact by employing striking comparisons or contrasts. These methods can underscore your point and prompt new perspectives and behaviors. Strengthen your comparisons by highlighting unexpected similarities between two seemingly different things. For instance, a finance leader used graphs of a heart attack and a stock market crash to emphasize the importance of addressing economic issues. Alternatively, utilize contrast to emphasize the distinctions between preferred and unpreferred options. Avoid undermining positive information with qualifiers like "but" or "however"; instead, present bad news followed by good news for a more effective delivery. When addressing weaknesses, place negative information just before a compelling argument to enhance persuasion. Finally, use contrast to highlight the silver lining in weaknesses, turning them into strengths. Employ comparisons and contrasts to bolster the persuasiveness of your points.

Secure a commitment

Encourage commitments and consistency by making them public, active, and voluntary. For example, a restaurant reduced no-shows by changing a reservation request from a statement to a question, resulting in a commitment to call if plans changed. To effectively utilize this approach: First, seek positive ways to prompt public, active, and voluntary commitments. Second, start with small commitments to pave the way for larger ones. Third, ask for specific details on when and how they will fulfill a commitment. Fourth, highlight progress to build momentum and demonstrate achievement. In a study, specifying when and where to do breast cancer checks resulted in 100% compliance compared to a general commitment. Acknowledge and showcase small wins to reinforce progress toward larger persuasive goals.

Ask for advice

Seek help or advice using the Benjamin Franklin influence method. Like Franklin, compliment and respect the person as you ask for input or assistance. Keep it simple, acknowledging their expertise and asking for their thoughts. Make it easy for them to say yes by requesting things that require minimal time or effort. Afterward, express genuine gratitude. Studies show that expressing gratitude significantly increases the likelihood of receiving assistance in the future. In one study, those who received thanks were more than twice as likely to provide further help compared to those who did not receive gratitude. Another study with fundraisers demonstrated a 50% increase in calls when they received genuine thanks. Follow these guidelines, be open about seeking help, and express gratitude sincerely for mutual benefit.

Appeal to high-level goals

Align your influence efforts with organizational strategy and high-level goals to enhance your impact and career prospects. Avoid being perceived as narrow-minded by demonstrating awareness and concern for broader contributions beyond your job description. To implement this approach: First, understand your organization's strategy and top-priority goals at all hierarchical levels above your direct responsibility. Second, showcase a mindset that extends beyond your job title, emphasizing a broader perspective. Third, illustrate how your proposals contribute to the organization's strategy or crucial performance goals beyond your immediate tasks, encompassing larger teams, units, functions, or the organization as a whole. Connecting your influence objectives to strategic priorities will not only strengthen your argument but also elevate your professional standing.

Social proof

Leverage social proof, especially in uncertain conditions, by appealing to others in similar situations to guide decision-making. Historical examples, such as paid opera applauders, demonstrate the long-standing influence of social proof. To apply this principle effectively: First, highlight trends in opinion or behavior through surveys, polls, or purchase rates that align with the desired outcome. Second, provide testimonials or success stories from individuals, teams, or organizations resembling the target audience. Third, be cautious of negative social proof, as drawing attention to undesirable behaviors can backfire. Carefully utilize social proof to showcase positive examples and encourage the desired behavior in those you seek to influence.

Reciprocity

To enhance reciprocation, follow Ivan Misner's advice: "The best way to get what you want is to help others get what they want." Effective favors have three key qualities: they are personalized, meaningful, and unexpected. For instance, a study on restaurant servers showed that leaving one mint increased tips by 3.3%, while two mints raised tips by 14.4%. The impact heightened to 23% when the unexpected element was emphasized by giving the mints sequentially. Favors don't need to be large or costly; their structure matters most. Take these steps: First, provide value to those you want to influence before seeking anything in return. Second, ensure your acts of kindness are personalized, meaningful, and unexpected. Proactively initiate reciprocation.

The power of gratitude

Learn from influential individuals by adopting the habit of expressing gratitude regularly. Utilize the "power thank you" method, consisting of thanking the person for a specific action, recognizing their effort, and explaining the impact on your life and your future actions. Try this with a role model influencer and witness its positive effects. Research indicates that just two minutes of gratitude can positively alter brain chemistry for the entire day.

Chapter 7 Communicating about Culturally Sensitive Issues

Same situation, different viewpoints

Navigating cultural differences can be complex, as individuals, influenced by various demographic and personal factors, often perceive issues differently. Elements such as religion, age, race, gender, sexual orientation, nationality, ability status, ethnicity, and language shape our perspectives. In contentious situations, people tend to defend their positions, akin to the example of Alfred and Mateo seeing different numbers in an image. The key, as suggested by Stephen Covey's fifth habit, is to prioritize understanding over being understood. Rather than changing perspectives, the goal is mutual respect and understanding in culturally sensitive conversations. The approach involves making a genuine effort to comprehend the other person's viewpoint, fostering a better understanding for both parties.

Implicit associations and unconscious bias

Bias, whether positive or negative, involves unconscious judgments and associations. While these biases are innate, they become problematic when unrecognized, influencing decisions and perceptions in ways that may harm individuals. The story serves as a reminder of how unconscious bias can affect our thinking. Acknowledging everyone's biases, including our own, is the first step toward understanding and addressing them. Resources like Project Implicit offer tests to explore implicit biases related to various characteristics, fostering self-awareness and challenging assumptions. The key is to recognize biases, question assumptions, and strive for a more informed and unbiased perspective.

Avoid microaggressions

Microaggressions in the workplace function like drops of water on an electronic device. While one may seem harmless, the cumulative effect can be damaging. Microaggressions are subtle insults that convey negative messages and, when unaddressed, can lead to frustration and alienation. For instance, questioning someone's origin based on their ethnicity, as seen in the example, can make them feel like an outsider. Other common microaggressions include selective eye contact in meetings and making assumptions about someone's abilities based on their race. When someone shares their experience of a microaggression, it's crucial not to minimize or invalidate it. Instead, acknowledge the impact, respond empathetically, and recognize the potential harm caused by the accumulation of such experiences in the workplace.

Ground rules for culturally sensitive conversations

When anticipating a potentially heated conversation, establish ground rules to maintain a productive dialogue. Disagreement is acceptable, but being disagreeable is not. Four recommended rules are approaching with an open mind, avoiding stereotypes, having the courage to embrace discomfort, and acknowledging triggers. Recognize that diverse opinions exist, so approach conversations with openness, listen without comparing to personal ideas, and understand perspectives without necessarily agreeing. Avoid stereotypes, as they hinder treating individuals based on their merits. Acknowledge that culturally sensitive discussions may be uncomfortable but require courage. If discomfort becomes overwhelming, agree to communicate triggers and either shift the topic or end the conversation, respecting each other's boundaries. Establishing such guidelines promotes constructive communication in challenging conversations.

Focus on impact rather than intent

In conversations about culturally sensitive topics, there is a common tendency to emphasize a person's intentions over the impact of their words or actions. While intentions matter, the focus should remain on the actual impact to foster productive discussions. This is evident in physical harm situations, where the intent versus impact discussion is straightforward. For instance, if someone spills hot tea on you accidentally, their good intentions do not negate the burn or stain you suffer. The challenge arises in non-physical manifestations of harm, especially in discussions about culturally sensitive issues. When offensive comments are made, it is crucial to prioritize the acknowledgment of emotional or psychological pain caused, rather than dwelling excessively on the offender's intentions. Just as one would address physical harm sincerely, recognizing impact promotes more constructive conversations and avoids unproductive judgments or labeling.

Commit to a dialogue rather than debate

When confronted with differing opinions, especially on culturally divisive topics, the inclination is often to engage in debate, aiming to prove one's perspective as right. However, fostering open, honest, and respectful dialogue is more constructive. Mark Gerzon, in "Leading Through Conflict," distinguishes between debate and dialogue. In debates, participants strive to prove the other side wrong, defending their own viewpoint. Conversely, dialogue involves collaborative efforts to reach a common understanding, acknowledging that perspectives can be enriched by diverse views. Debating often involves looking for flaws in others' arguments, potentially delegitimizing their experiences. In a dialogue, the focus is on understanding different perspectives without dismissing lived experiences. While debate aims for a winner and loser, dialogue seeks common ground, allowing for ongoing engagement and clearer understanding of issues. While debates have their place, culturally sensitive topics benefit more from a dialogue approach, fostering healthy discussions and maintaining relationships.

Remember that words matter

Children are often taught that words cannot hurt as much as physical actions, but in reality, words can be deeply hurtful. Language evolves, and what was once acceptable may now be offensive. While intentions matter, the impact of words is significant, regardless of intent. To promote inclusive communication, consider using people-first language for those with disabilities, removing gender from roles, limiting profanity in professional settings, and avoiding slurs and derogatory phrases. Be cautious about using historically offensive language, even if some groups have reclaimed it, and recognize the responsibility we all have for the words we choose.

Use the platinum rule

While the golden rule advises treating others as you want to be treated, it assumes everyone shares the same preferences. This normalization can be problematic, especially in diverse cultural contexts. The platinum rule suggests treating people as they want to be treated, acknowledging and respecting individual differences. For instance, in work scenarios, understanding colleagues' preferences can improve communication and collaboration. Instead of assuming everyone celebrates the same holidays, as in the Christmas example, practicing the platinum rule involves building relationships, learning colleagues' preferences, and adjusting interactions accordingly. Upgrade from the golden to platinum rule by valuing and respecting the diverse perspectives and preferences of those around you.

Be an ally for those around you

Facing the vast conflicts rooted in cultural differences can be overwhelming, prompting individuals to question their impact. A potent way to contribute to diversity and inclusion efforts is by becoming an ally. An ally aligns with initiatives to enhance conditions for marginalized or disadvantaged groups. Being an ally involves intentional actions, such as speaking out against inappropriate behavior and actively learning about others' experiences. It requires humility, emphasizing listening over speaking, and acknowledging one's privilege. Allies don't need to fix problems but play a crucial role in fostering diversity and inclusion by demonstrating empathy and yielding their privilege. Privilege, unearned benefits, should be acknowledged without guilt, and allies actively work to create a more equitable environment.

Respond with empathy

When someone shares a challenging experience, the common instinct is to offer advice, question, criticize, or show empathy. An empathetic response, characterized by focused listening, validating feelings, and offering support, is the most effective, especially when cultural aspects are involved. Avoid questioning the person's account, as it may convey distrust. Being critical can be perceived as blaming the victim, exacerbating the situation. Providing unsolicited advice is often unhelpful unless explicitly requested. Choose a simple and empathetic response to foster a supportive connection.

How to ask questions about culturally sensitive topics

When facing uncertainty about diversity-related matters, it is crucial to avoid silence, which can convey unintended messages and lead to future problems. Instead, ask respectful and genuinely interested questions. Many people either shy away from asking due to discomfort or approach it in a rude or judgmental manner, damaging relationships. When posing questions, avoid public settings that single out individuals and be cautious about asking someone to represent an entire group. Privately inquire about an individual's experience, expressing a genuine interest in understanding. For example, ask if they are comfortable discussing a specific topic and seek insights into their personal experiences. This approach humanizes the issue and alleviates the burden of representation. If asked to discuss a topic and you are uncomfortable, politely decline, emphasizing that you appreciate their interest. When engaging in such conversations, be gracious and understanding, recognizing the learning curve for those unfamiliar with certain issues. Additionally, acknowledge that you are sharing your own lived experience, not representing everyone in your demographic. Avoiding uncomfortable questions stifles progress and hinders productivity at various levels. Embrace curiosity, ask questions privately, and be receptive to the responses, respecting others' comfort levels in discussing certain topics.

How to share feedback that you're insulted

Inevitably, colleagues may say or do things that are frustrating or offensive. Unproductive responses include staying silent and harboring negative feelings, talking to others instead of the person involved, or confronting them in the moment. To respond more productively, give yourself time to process the incident. Share your frustration with a trusted mentor or write out your feelings for therapeutic purposes, ensuring it is not left lying around. Consider the offender's role and your working relationship, determining if it impacts productivity. If feedback is necessary, carefully choose your words, schedule a private discussion, and focus on facts, feelings, and future behavior. Personalize feedback by using "I" statements and describing specific behaviors, avoiding accusations. Stick to specifics and communicate your feelings to diffuse tension during this uncomfortable but important conversation.

Ways to apologize

Despite our best efforts, everyone makes mistakes, and it is likely we'll offend or insult someone at work. A study from Ohio State University identifies six components of an effective apology: acknowledge responsibility, offer to repair the issue, express regret, explain what went wrong, repent for the problem, and request forgiveness. Acknowledging responsibility is crucial, especially when apologizing to someone with a different viewpoint. Ignoring the situation or making light of it can worsen matters. Avoid defensive excuses, "ifs" and "buts," and dismissive apologies. Instead, focus on the action, avoid qualifiers, and use language that takes responsibility for the impact of your statement or action. A genuine apology sets the foundation for moving forward and helps maintain your personal brand.

Improve your communication skills

Avoiding open discussions on cultural topics hinders progress, a pattern that has persisted for centuries. While the saying "A closed mouth never has a foot in it" holds some truth, a global workforce cannot reach its full potential without cross-cultural conversations. Fear of negative labels often leads to silence, but it is acceptable to make mistakes. If you unintentionally misspeak, refer to effective apologies. Making errors does not define you; it is an opportunity for improvement. Regularly applying the communication tips will make it easier, and your commitment to enhancing these skills is a positive step forward.

Chapter 8 Communicating with Emotional Intelligence

What is emotional intelligence?

Emotional intelligence, defined by the Institute for Health and Human Potential, involves recognizing emotions' impact on behavior, learning to manage them, and understanding others' emotions under pressure. Author Travis Bradberry describes emotional intelligence as "the other kind of smart," distinguishing it from technical skills and intelligence. EQ comprises four categories: self-awareness, acknowledging strengths and weaknesses; self-regulation, managing emotions and life; empathy, understanding others' perspectives; and relationship management, fostering connections and offering support. To enhance your EQ, observe examples of emotional intelligence around you and learn from individuals who excel in self-awareness, self-regulation, empathy, and relationship management.

Why emotional intelligence matters

Research consistently supports the positive impact of EI on organizational performance and individual success. Studies across various professions, including healthcare, accounting, and office work, demonstrate the correlation between EI and job performance. In a study of a global food and beverage company, senior managers with high EI capabilities exceeded yearly earning goals by 20%, earning substantial bonuses. Conversely, executives lacking EI received less favorable reviews. Customer interactions, influenced by emotional intelligence, significantly impact business success. Research by Porath and Pearson reveals that perceived rudeness from employees diminishes customer trust and willingness to make purchases. While strong analytical abilities contribute to profit, partners with high social skills (EI) added 110% more incremental profit than those with less social skills. The Center for Creative Leadership estimates that 75% of career derailments result from deficiencies in emotional competencies. Strengthening your emotional intelligence is crucial for career success, even though people often overestimate their EI skills.

Communicate confidently and with thoughtfulness

Conversational style significantly influences how people perceive emotional intelligence. A study at Cornell University, analyzing nearly 1300 online conversations, distinguished between diplomatic discussions with opposing views and those descending into hostility or hurt feelings. To enhance emotional intelligence in difficult conversations, replace danger phrases with thoughtful alternatives. Prioritize understanding the other person's perspective, express gratitude, and avoid defensive "why" or leading questions. Replace trivializing responses with acknowledgment and timely replies. When sharing your viewpoint, use tentative statements, avoiding absolute assertions. Provide constructive feedback by assuming positive intent and avoiding blame. Start sentences with "I" or "we" to avoid sounding accusatory. Embrace emotionally intelligent communication strategies for mutual understanding rather than winning. Choose one strategy to practice until it becomes natural in your conversations.

Manage your emotions

Learn to self-regulate your emotions in challenging situations to avoid projecting your feelings through facial expressions. Change your thoughts to alter your emotions; for example, shift from boredom to finding a positive aspect. When faced with provocative statements, focus on controlled breathing, break eye contact, and take notes to quiet internal chatter. Imagine channeling the calmest person you know, adopting a neutral expression. Relax facial muscles, shoulders, and arms for a composed appearance. Build a delay between thoughts and speech, using sips of water to swallow regrettable words. Respond calmly with neutral phrases, like "Tell me more" or "I'm not sure," buying time when needed. Practice these techniques to enhance emotional intelligence and be recognized for staying calm in any situation.

Understand others' views

Boost your empathic imagination through the "five innocent reasons" game, re-sequencing events, and reading literary fiction. Interactions play a crucial role, and scheduling phone calls enhances empathic accuracy. Actively engage with diverse thinkers to combat the echo chamber effect, promoting understanding of different perspectives. Incorporate these five strategies into your routine to build empathy and better comprehend others.

Switch perspectives

Three colleagues were complaining about a parking issue at the office. While venting, Tom suggested a different perspective, noting that the David likely did not intentionally choose the inconvenient timing. This shift in viewpoint transformed their feelings from frustration to understanding. Positive or toxic cultures often stem from such perspective shifts. Tom's comment served as a game-changer, emphasizing the importance of assuming the best rather than assuming the worst.

Balance empathy and accountability

When your colleague Amanda makes a significant mistake with repercussions for your work, it is crucial to balance empathy and accountability. Start by discussing expectations before issues arise, ensuring clear communication. Remember that you can empathize and disagree; understanding someone's feelings does not imply endorsing their behavior. Listen to Amanda's perspective, paraphrase to show understanding, and express your feelings with vulnerability, such as saying, "I'm worried this could impact my relationship with my boss." Differentiate between cognitive and affective empathy; you can understand Amanda's experience without internalizing her distress. Strive for a balanced culture that combines high empathy with high accountability, as leaders with high empathy are more likely to set expectations and address performance issues effectively.

Showing you're listening

To truly demonstrate effective listening, it is not just about being attentive; your body language matters. Sit up, lean in, and maintain eye contact to convey engagement. Adjust your camera for clear visibility during video conferences. Nod slowly to indicate attentive listening, and consciously relax your eyebrows, aiming for a 20% smile to avoid unintentional signs of anger. Steer clear of distractions like phones during conversations, as snubbing others for your device can diminish perceived communication skills and empathy. Practice tuning into the body language and facial expressions of others, whether in-person or virtually, to enhance emotional intelligence. Focus on nonverbal cues such as eye contact, tone of voice, and seating arrangements to gain a deeper understanding of others. Utilize resources like watching TV with the volume off or taking facial expression quizzes to hone your ability to read and empathize with others.

Paraphrase messages in your response

According to Brene Brown, connection is more effective than trying to fix things. Paraphrasing is a powerful way to show empathy—summarizing both content and emotion in your own words. Practice paraphrasing in different scenarios, making sure to avoid negating feelings or attempting to fix the situation. Empathetic responses, like paraphrasing, demonstrate understanding and care. Practice paraphrasing daily to enhance your empathetic communication skills.

Chapter 9 Writing Email

Write to your audience

When writing an email, consider your audience. Tailor the level of detail and formality based on your relationship with the recipient. Formality is crucial when corresponding with customers, including a proper salutation and sign-off. Avoid jargon and use explanatory language for customers. Provide a clear message with a call to action. For instance, a formal customer email might offer a discount and encourage booking an appointment. Adjust your approach based on the recipient's preferences and your relationship with them. Note the importance of understanding how your audience uses email, considering factors like age or preferred communication platforms. In a larger organization, be mindful of diverse email practices among coworkers and adapt your communication style accordingly.

Identify your purpose

Every work email serves a purpose, whether explicit, like scheduling a meeting, or subtle, like relationship-building. Common reasons include sharing information, seeking answers, assigning tasks, summarizing meetings, creating records, and marketing. Clearly state the main point early in the message to increase visibility. For example, when asking a question, place it at the beginning, providing context for better understanding. For longer emails, especially meeting summaries, highlight the purpose and use formatting to enhance readability. Soften the delivery of bad news with a positive or friendly opening. Understand both immediate and broader purposes to align with company values. Knowing your email's purpose guides effective communication and helps determine the appropriate communication channel—email, text, or phone call.

Keep related messages together

Take advantage of email's organizational benefits by starting new threads for distinct topics. While email allows easy tracking of message history, threads can deviate from their initial purpose. For clarity, initiate separate threads for each idea or project, making it simpler for readers to manage their messages. When discussions shift within a thread, consider starting a new email to maintain organization. For instance, if a conversation on vendors evolves into details about a company event, create a new thread with a message like, "Let's begin a separate thread for the event discussion to keep everything organized." This practice enhances communication and earns appreciation from recipients.

Write effective subject lines

Crafting effective emails requires careful consideration of the subject line, a crucial element that determines whether your message is opened or overlooked. When creating a subject line, prioritize clarity, brevity, and specificity to convey the main idea efficiently. Avoid generic terms and opt for detailed subject lines, as research indicates they have higher open rates. For instance, when promoting a limited-time offer, use a specific subject like "15% Off Hair Cuts—Book by Friday." Tailor your approach based on your audience and their email habits. Keep subject lines between 30 and 60 characters for optimal visibility, considering variations on different devices. Additionally, pay attention to preview text, ensuring it complements the subject line and provides a snapshot of the email's content. Be cautious with misleading preview text and avoid clickbait phrases, as professionalism enhances the likelihood of engagement. Regularly review and refine your subject lines to align with your email's actual content, ensuring clarity and effectiveness.

Use direct openings

To ensure your email meets expectations set by the subject line and preview text, be direct and concise in the message. For instance, if the subject line is "Please Confirm Hair Cut Appointment," the email's opening should provide all necessary details for confirmation without diverting to unrelated topics. If additional information is essential, consider sending a separate message later. In another scenario, when giving feedback on an investor proposal, avoid unnecessary details and focus on specific requests. Instead of a vague and rambling message, provide clear instructions, such as relocating a section and adding a table, with a deadline for the next draft. Direct openings ensure clarity, avoid ambiguity, and facilitate effective communication.

Highlight action items

In emails, when seeking action from the recipient, it is crucial to emphasize the request. Begin by hinting at the action needed in the subject line, using tags like "Action needed" or more specific wording. Place your request at the beginning of the email to catch the reader's attention. Clearly state what you want, how you want it (e.g., using track changes), and by when (e.g., Friday at 2:00). If there are multiple action items, number or use bullets to highlight them. When emailing multiple recipients with different tasks, assign names to each action item, putting each on a new line with bolded names. Additionally, make it explicit when no action is required. Keep action items at the top, especially in lengthy emails, and consider highlighting names for better visibility. Clearly outlining action items increases the likelihood of successful and timely responses.

Structure your message for easy reading

Effective formatting is crucial in emails as it enhances readability and underscores professionalism. Begin with a professional greeting and, if appropriate, a short, friendly opening line. Keep your opening concise, directly stating the purpose of your message. Use short paragraphs or single-line information to capture attention, as lengthy emails may lead to skimming and missed points. For longer emails, employ subheadings, bolded text, and lists to enhance readability. Use bold or italics sparingly to emphasize critical points. Avoid excessive use of unusual fonts or colored text. When sharing links, embed them in descriptive text rather than pasting the whole URL. Give meaningful names to attachments for easy identification. Thoughtful formatting ensures clarity, engagement, and a higher likelihood of receiving the desired responses.

End strong

End your email on a positive note by expressing gratitude or a positive statement. If your email is lengthy, gently restate your request. Choose a professional sign-off such as best regards, sincerely, or thank you, aligning with your corporate culture. Include a standard email signature with your title and contact details, promoting any relevant items judiciously. Customize signature blocks for different recipients, tailoring information based on their needs. Avoid adding offensive or off-putting elements to your signature. Use the closing to leave a favorable impression and provide the necessary information for future communication.

Find the right tone

Written communication, while efficient, is prone to misinterpretation due to the absence of vocal and visual cues. Consider the recipient's familiarity and past interactions to determine an appropriate tone. If the person uses a casual tone, mirroring it can help build rapport. Regardless of the relationship, starting with a correctly spelled name adds a personal touch. Tailor the formality of your greeting accordingly, such as "Dear Ms. Montes" or "Hi Anderson." Strike a balance in tone, avoiding excessive informality or abruptness. Responding positively and avoiding unnecessary criticism fosters a productive environment. Refrain from sending emails in a negative emotional state; wait until you have calmed down. Elements like greetings, emojis, and sentence length contribute to tone. Politeness, including "please" and "thank you," enhances communication. Ultimately, prioritize making recipients feel valued, supported, and respected to cultivate positive professional relationships.

Use appropriate punctuation and styles

Text formatting and punctuation significantly impact the tone of an email. While bold and italics can emphasize words or headings, excessive use may seem unprofessional. All caps are generally perceived as shouting and are rarely suitable in professional emails. The role of exclamation points varies across generations, with younger individuals often using more for positivity and enthusiasm. Consider your audience's preferences; some may find exclamation points genuine, while others view them as unprofessional. In professional emails, it's advisable to include periods, even though informal contexts often omit them. Multiple punctuation marks, especially in a row, can convey a demanding or panicked tone, so use them judiciously to ensure your intended tone is conveyed. Understanding your audience's perceptions of formatting and punctuation choices enhances effective communication.

Personalize your message

Personalizing your message is crucial for effective communication, considering factors such as your audience's familiarity, potential reactions, and desired actions. Whether addressing colleagues, clients, or investors, tailor your tone and content accordingly. For employees, convey details warmly and informally, expressing gratitude for their hard work. Clients benefit from informative yet enthusiastic messages, emphasizing the new location's perks and offering incentives. Investors receive a more formal announcement, expressing gratitude for their support. By customizing your emails to meet each group's needs, you ensure clear communication and a positive response.

Proofread your message

Avoid the embarrassment of typos and errors in your emails by implementing thorough proofreading techniques. Take your time to review the message, considering tricks to see it with fresh eyes. Reading aloud or using text-to-speech tools helps identify errors. Changing the text's appearance by altering font, color, or size can also aid in catching mistakes. If the email is crucial, print it out for a different perspective. Separate proofreading tasks, focusing on punctuation and spelling individually. Leverage digital tools like spell checkers and grammar checkers, but scrutinize their suggestions. Utilize autocorrect for common mistypes and pay special attention to names. Consider enabling the delay send feature to allow for last-minute corrections. For vital or challenging emails, seek input from a colleague to ensure clarity and tone. Thoughtful proofreading ensures error-free, polished communication that reflects positively on you and your company.

Respect confidentiality

Remember that emails are not as private as they may seem. Employers can access your messages, and security breaches or legal issues could expose them. Be cautious about what you write, especially regarding colleagues or sensitive company matters. Avoid accidental disclosures by using the "reply all" function sparingly, and double-check recipients in group emails. Protect confidential information, such as client data or proprietary business details. If a message would not be acceptable to a wide audience, reconsider sending it. For sensitive information, consider discussing it in person or over the phone instead of via email. Understanding the lack of complete privacy in emails and following these guidelines helps prevent unintended disclosures and safeguards sensitive data.

Forward email with care

Forwarding emails can be convenient for adding new people to a conversation, but it comes with potential issues, particularly regarding confidentiality. Before forwarding, consider if the new recipient needs to see the entire email chain and if it is necessary to include contact information. Delete unnecessary details to preserve confidentiality and reduce overwhelming content. Clearly explain why you are forwarding the email and include your thoughts and action items. When uncertain, seek permission before forwarding sensitive information and explicitly mention it in your message to establish trust. Careful selection and framing of forwarded messages contribute to clear, respectful communication and demonstrate trustworthiness.

Copying and blind copying

The term "CC" in email originates from "carbon copy," a practice where copies were made using carbon paper. In modern email systems, the "To" field lists primary recipients, and the "CC" (carbon copy) field includes individuals being copied for information. Recipients in the "CC" field are visible to all, indicating those not central to the email's focus. "BCC" (blind carbon copy) secretly sends copies without revealing recipients' email addresses. This is useful for privacy or when addressing a large group. While CC and BCC have benefits, overuse or misuse can lead to drawbacks, such as unnecessary inclusions or actions that may appear sneaky. Practicing caution and understanding these distinctions ensures professional and respectful email communication.

Taking conversations offline

While email is a valuable tool, it is not always the most suitable choice for communication. Long messages may indicate the need for a more interactive discussion via phone, video call, or in-person meeting. When multiple participants are involved or communication issues arise, an offline approach is often more effective. Delivering bad news, discussing sensitive matters, or seeking immediate responses may be better handled through alternative means like phone calls or text messages. Additionally, occasional non-email communication methods, such as phone or video chats, can strengthen relationships. The optimal communication method depends on the specific context and goals of the situation.

Use email for good

Email does not have to be dull; it can be a tool for expressing gratitude and building connections. Take a moment to thank others for their work, friendship, or support. A sincere and brief thank-you email can make someone's day. Be specific about what you are grateful for and why it matters. For instance, express appreciation for someone covering your shift in a time of need or for their understanding in challenging situations. Consider using the CC field to share your thanks publicly and strengthen relationships. Remember, email is not just for business; it is a means to foster both professional and personal connections. Show respect and gratitude, and you will contribute to a more positive world.

www.ingramcontent.com/pod-product-compliance
Lightning Source LLC
Chambersburg PA
CBHW062301290526
45794CB00006B/2650